Made in the USA
Coppell, TX
21 October 2021

64261816R10068

Made in the USA
Las Vegas, NV
08 June 2021

24402873R00073

This book belongs to

____